IMAGES OF ENGLAND

Around
Stocksbridge

The Clock Tower. This familiar landmark was built between 1920 and 1923 as a War Memorial. The tower itself was funded by public subscription on land granted by R.H.R. Rimington-Wilson. The impressive steps, once affording a short cut from Manchester Road to Bocking Hill, eventually fell into disrepair and were removed.

IMAGES OF ENGLAND

Around Stocksbridge

Stocksbridge & District History Society

NONSUCH

Billeting at STOCKSBRIDGE

Billeting at Stocksbridge. Although there is a light-hearted message hand-written on the back, inviting Harold to come and stay in Stocksbridge at Easter, we do not know who sent it or when. The figures depicted are not military types, so perhaps it relates to a period when many were seeking work and lodgings here – possibly in the post-General Strike period of 1930.

First published 1995
This new pocket edition 2006
Images unchanged from first edition

Nonsuch Publishing Limited
The Mill, Brimscombe Port,
Stroud, Gloucestershire, GL5 2QG
www.nonsuch-publishing.com

Nonsuch Publishing is an imprint of Tempus Publishing Group

British Library Cataloguing in Publication Data.
A catalogue record for this book is available from the British Library.

ISBN 1-84588-322-5

Typesetting and origination by Nonsuch Publishing Limited
Printed in Great Britain by Oaklands Book Services Limited

Contents

We dedicate this book to local historians past, present and future, and to all who may be intrigued by such a photograph and feel compelled to try to discover its origin. It has been suggested that the machine could be a horse-drawn gin, such as the one once in use at Langley Brook Farm.

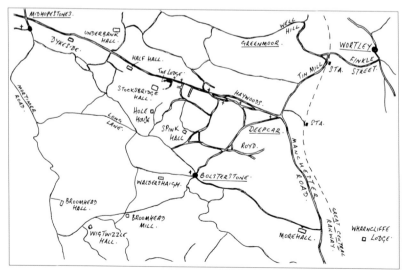

Stocksbridge and District, c1900.

Introduction

Less than 200 years ago the only inhabitants of the Little Don and Ewden valleys were mainly agricultural workers; the only buildings scattered smallholdings and farms attached to the manor houses of minor gentry, cottages of blacksmiths and stonemasons and the churches which served the village communities. The earliest signs of industry, cornmills using the water power of the two rivers, were also dependent on the products of the land. The 1851 census shows that the majority of employment was still on the land, although by then coal had been discovered and mining became the next largest occupation. Many small outcrops were worked as well as deeper shafts. Lead had been worked in the Bitholmes and Ewden until exhausted, but now clays were also discovered.

The Industrial Revolution brought much needed employment to the area and we find that our farm workers turned their hands to new skills, but had to compete with a tremendous influx of people from all over the country, attracted by the opportunities of employment in the steel, brick and building industries established here. Within thirty years the population had increased five-fold.

Shops were opened to supply the growing population and what had been beer-houses attached to farms or smithies became public houses and inns serving new roads. There was more employment for carters and builders and a need for more schools.

The agricultural depression caused more hardship for those still dependent on the land, and some farms were abandoned, while some disappeared under new reservoirs. Those that survive are among the oldest buildings in the area, and although many have been restored to provide modern housing, some are still in a ruinous state. A few remain as working farms.

Village communities have existed at Bolsterstone, Deepcar, Wortley, Midhope and Langsett for centuries. Only with the growth of industry in the Don valley did the town of Stocksbridge grow from a group of only seven households clustered around Stocks Bridge in 1850 to the vast sprawl which has now all but absorbed its parent villages.

The photographs we have selected date mainly from the end of the nineteenth and the beginning of the twentieth centuries, and show how the area has changed and developed. Our way of life is no longer the entirely church-based society that it was a hundred years ago, and we hope this book will be, for many readers, a nostalgic reminder of our parents' and grandparents' time.

Acknowledgements

We acknowledge the co-operation of Sheffield City Library in granting permission to use Archive material and we thank all those who have provided photographs and information to aid our research.

We would also like to mention the photographers, most of them household names: Biltcliffe, Bradbury, Broadbent, G. Dawson, A. Elson, Howson, Sheldon, and H. Whittaker, without their enthusiasm very little record would survive of the activities of our forebears.

One

Around the Valleys

Wigtwizzle Hall. Mary, daughter of the Rev. John Ibbotson of Wigtwizzle, married Christopher Wilson of Broomhead Hall in 1623. It was demolished in 1923 and the stone was used to build the Waterboard houses near Morehall. Some gateposts can still be seen in the wall opposite Wigtwizzle Cottages.

Bolsterstone, the parent village. Castle Cottage on the left was built around what remains of the Manor House. In the southern elevation can be seen mullioned windows, the join with lighter stone visible on the left. The finials on the church tower, seen here faintly above the cottage extension, have been removed.

Bolsterstone Porter's Lodge. The building now accepted to have been the porter's lodge to the Manor House, as it was when occupied as a dwelling. Hannah Parkin, a widowed pauper, lived there in 1851, and the place was known as Hannah Parkin's Cottage. Later it was used as a reading room, then a base for the Church Youth Club, and most recently as a changing room for the Stocksbridge Rugby Club.

Broomhead Hall. Built in 1640 by Christopher Wilson, who had turned down the chance of a knighthood by declining his invitation to the coronation of Charles I. Later he became a captain in the Parliamentary Army. This later building was the design of James Rimington, already very much out of date. It was demolished in 1980, but the Broomhead Farm Estate is still very much a going concern.

Broomhead Mill Farm. Farmer James Crofts and his wife Annie, their daughters Mrs Annie Elizabeth Shaw, Ellen and Lily Crofts, a cousin and little Mabel Shaw. The site is now submerged under Broomhead Reservoir.

Dykeside Farm and 'Lepping' Stones, Midhope. Joseph Hill's House is now submerged under Underbank Reservoir.

Underbank Hall. The building is of sixteenth-century origin. It was occupied by landowners Wests, Fentons and lastly deWend Fentons. The farm was tenanted in the mid-1800s by the Thompson family who had been evicted from Wigtwizzle when the property was sold. Underbank was used from 1959 by BSC for entertaining visiting VIPs. The farm buildings have now been converted into private dwellings.

Half Hall, Stocksbridge. In the 1774 Waldershelf Window Bill it was listed as How Fall and was taxed for seven windows. The 1871 Census returns recorded it as Hauve Hall. James Hattersley occupied it in 1851 and his son was still there in 1891, one of the few farms to stay in the same family throughout that period. The Silver Fox public house now stands on the site.

HALF HALL, STOCKSBRIDGE.

Horner House. Believed to have been named by one John Horner. The 1662 date stone now is part of Newton Grange boundary wall. There were two farms and a cottage with thirty acres of land including a penfold. The Broadheads acquired it from Amos Ridal and it has been used as a joiner's shop, a bakery and a slaughterhouse. The last occupants were Harry Newton and sons. The whole area became known as Horner House and still is, although the original farmstead has been demolished.

Stocksbridge Hall. Built in 1858 by Amos Ridal on Horner House land and occupied by him until after 1871. In 1881 it housed Dr Ward from Penistone and has been almost continuously since then a doctors' surgery and home.

The Lodge, Park Drive, also known as Gate Lodge, was the only local casualty of German bombing in World War Two. This photograph is dated to 1915.

Spink Hall. The original house was built by Ralph Ellis of Midhope Hall in the early 1600s, occupied by Henry Hodgkinson, doctor and master of Bolsterstone School. The Middle House on the right was built in 1833 with the farmhouse and farm buildings behind. The Top House on the left and a carriage house were added in 1866-8 by John Grayson. There is an entrance to a tunnel, supposed to lead to Bolsterstone, in the farm buildings. The stable once housed twenty horses. This photograph was taken in Mrs Askew's time. The hollies by the main door are still there.

Waldershaigh, Bolsterstone. Built for Charles Macro Wilson in the 1860s by John Brearley. C.M. Wilson bought back the Wilson MSS and built the cairn on Walderslow, which he believed is the burial place of a Saxon chieftain. The Rev. William Reginald Wilson occupied Waldershaigh after his brother's death. Later it became the property of the Bruce family. Bolsterstone Girl Guides occasionally met there under Mrs Margaret Cobbe in the 1940s.

Ewden village. Built to house immigrant workers on Broomhead Reservoirs, this was a model village and people came from all over the country to inspect its facilities. Families whose menfolk had worked on Howden dams at Derwent settled here, moving into Bolsterstone, Deepcar and Stocksbridge as the work finished. Gradually the houses have disappeared. One was still functioning as a Youth Hostel in 1965. The railway which brought materials up from the main line at Morehall can be seen in the foreground.

Morehall/Moorhall/Moorehall. The More family dates back to pre-Norman times but had died out by the time the Dragon of Wantley ballad was written. This most recent building was sixteenth-century. In 1691 Nicholas Stead of Onesacre, gentleman, bought Moorehall from George Fox, paying the Lord of the Manor a yearly rent of one red rose. In 1861 it was occupied by the Rev. John Bell, curate of Bolsterstone, and later by Charles Macro Wilson. The east wing, on the right, is the oldest part surviving, along with the farmhouse beyond, which has a window of Bolsterstone glass, and the fifteenth century cruck barn.

Wharncliffe Lodge. Built by Sir Thomas Wortley in 1510, destroying two hamlets called Stanfield and Whitley to extend his chase. It was this, and Sir Richard Wortley's action seventy-nine years later in enlarging and enclosing his park, which caused violent opposition and inspired the satirical ballad 'The Dragon of Wantley'. James I created Sir Francis Wortley a baron and he fought for the King in the Civil War. On the losing side, he was captured and died in prison. The estate was restored and remains in the family. It is said that from the lodge one can see five counties.

Wharncliffe Crags. On the edge of the Wortley Estate, where in 1252 a grant of free warren enabled the lord of the manor to create a hunting chase. There is a cave known as the Dragon's Cave. Archaeologists have found evidence of iron-smelting in Roman times. On a lower shelf overlooking the confluence of the Little Don with the Don (in pre-history a swamp), was also found remains of a Mesolithic (Middle Stone Age) campsite. This card was posted to Matlock from Chester on Christmas Eve, 1903.

Deepcar from the Crags. Looking westward along Manchester Road to Stocksbridge and its smoking chimneys. The one in the right foreground belonged to an old corn-mill at the bottom of Vaughton Hill. At the junction with Haywoods Lane was once a blacking mill. The stacks of light coloured material on the right would have been brought down from Gregory's brickworks by 'Jinny' downhill on the left and through a culvert under the main road, which is still there.

Deepcar from Station Road. Florence Buildings in the near foreground were built for workers at Lowoods' Refractory. The River Don meets the Little Don here and because Florence Buildings were north of the river, they were in Penistone Parish. On the left is Mangle Row, so called because there actually was a mangle in the middle entry passage for common use. On the horizon is Gregory's brickworks factory chimney, erected 1891 and demolished exactly 100 years later.

Deepcar from Hunshelf. Gregory's chimney is on the left. The clough, later known as Fox Glen, runs from there along the tree-line. In the centre is Wood Royd. A viaduct had been built over the quarry which was later removed. At the bottom of Haywoods Lane, on the left, are allotments. Stubbin House Farm can be seen on the right.

New Haywoods. Housing built by Samuel Fox. Our cover picture was taken on one of these streets. There are allotments on the land between Haywood Lane and New Road, and also on land above Haywoods Park. The new vicarage stands alone on Bocking Hill. The next building above that is Watson House, and further still, the chimney of Brookes' pipeworks at Bracken Moor can be seen. Bolsterstone is on the left horizon, Spink Hall a little lower on the extreme right.

Stocksbridge Centre. St Matthias Church was built in 1890. The white house which stands out would be the manse built for the Methodist minister. Beyond the line of trees which mark the Clough is the newly built Garden City.

Stocksbridge from Hunshelf, c. 1920. Hole House Lane on the right derives its name from Hoyle House, which in turn developed from the local pronunciation of the original name of the Clough, the Hole. The chimney marks the pipe-works of William Brooke. The football pitch was on land belonging to Tom Batty of the Friendship Hotel, the building in the centre with a bay window. The field was later used for a market before being sold to the Department of Social Services and the Education Department. Victoria Street was only partly made up and there were steps at the top, with the Hollow Fields on the right.

Two

Grime and Graft

One of the oldest known photographs of the district taken in 1860 which shows how rapidly
Samuel Fox and Co. Ltd had developed in less than twenty years of operations. The Rising Sun
Inn can be seen on Hunshelf Bank and the cottage property in the foreground is still in use.

A pre-1923 view taken from Hunshelf Bank, showing a busy industrial scene. Note the carriages of Stocksbridge Railway Co. at the Low Yard terminus.

A panorama of the valley, c. 1920. Observers will note Brownhill Row located on Hunshelf Bank and a solitary motorized vehicle on the main road. Rimington Row in the foreground was built as back-to-back houses, the roadside premises used as shops. The property was eventually sold by John and James Rimington to Samuel Fox and Co. Ltd.

A continuation of the previous view showing the Siemens melting shop and a glimpse of the coke ovens which opened in 1918.

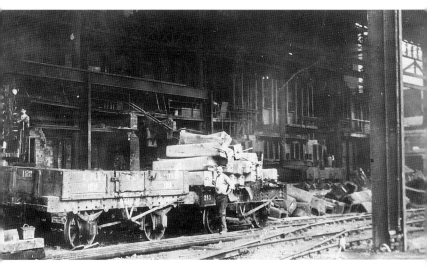

An early departmental view taken at an unknown location within Fox's Works. Such photographs are uncommon as there was no official Works photographer until the 1950s.

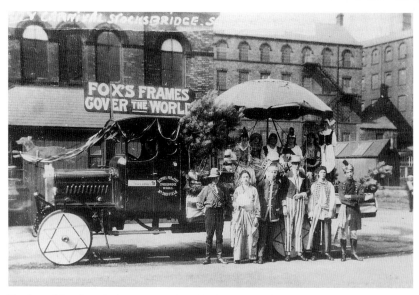

The Samuel Fox float which was on parade in the charity carnival on 12 September 1925. The frames referred to are of course umbrella frames

Another carnival float photographed outside Fox's factory. The multi-storey building on the right was the Umbrella Department.

S. Fox and Co. Ltd umbrella department. A view showing the bundling of ribs.

Spring Mill fitters of 1904. The laminated springs shown here were made for the railway industry initially, but the later development of road transport generated many new orders.

Pit strike at S. Fox and Co., 1911. The strike lasted for eleven months and achieved an increase in pay from seven to eight shillings a day. These miners went round playing the barrel organ to raise funds.

Coal outcropping during the miners strike of 1926.

A closer look at Stocksbridge Pit showing some tools of the trade and a rather forlorn looking pony. Note the extensive stocks of pit props and wheel sets for the tubs.

Ewden Valley Dam workers, c. 1922. Back row, left to right: Hatchett, Poppleton, F. Wood, Schofield and Stanley Duffield. Front row: Beaumont, Mate, -?-, -?-, -?-.

CHEMICAL WORKS
STOCKSBRIDGE

Above: The coke ovens. An early view of this section of the steelworks taken from Manchester Road. Production started in 1918, the coal being supplied by Fox's who took the coke, and Simon-Carves used the by-products.

Above: The Armitage Works Company Ltd. The Henholmes Works pictured here in 1890 had been established at least forty years earlier and were previously owned by Turner Brothers. The works thrived under the ownership and direction of John Armitage who died on 13 November 1890 aged 74 years.

Right: William Brooke and Sons. Known as Pot House Works and founded in 1902, they were located opposite the existing Stocksbridge Infants School on the Alpine Way. The photograph shows an interesting interior view and display of wares and appeared in Joseph Kenworthy's Handbook No. 4 published in 1915.

Opposite below: Hunshelf Corn Mill. The central area of this view is the site of the old Corn Mill which was built originally as a cloth mill in 1744. The adjacent properties are known as Corn Mill Cottages and look on to the Stocksbridge Railway. The very early locomotive shown dates the view to pre-1914.

Trade advertisements. This is a reproduction of the inside back cover of the Kenworthy Handbook referred to on the previous page and gives an insight into the extent of this type of industry in the area at the end of the nineteenth and the beginning of the twentieth centuries.

J. Grayson Lowood and Company Ltd. This is a wintry scene but the workmen do not wear winter clothes and so perhaps were warmed by their manual efforts in loading the wagons. Lowood Working Mens Club can be seen in the middle distance.

J. Grayson Lowood and Company Ltd. A group photograph taken in front of a kiln. The gentleman on the next to the front row (seventh from the left) is Mr John Helliwell who assisted in its construction

Deepcar industrial scene, showing just part of the thriving community in the early part of the twentieth century. 'Mangle Row' can be seen (extreme left) together with Florence Buildings (centre) and the chimney associated with Deepcar Corn Mill which was located at the bottom of Vaughton Hill.

Schofields Bottling Co. Ltd. This view dates back to approximately 1908 and was taken inside the Victoria Street premises at Stocksbridge. Adverts of the day relate to mineral waters, cordials, beers and stouts all being bottled on this site. Here we see a ferris wheel arrangement for cleaning the bottles.

Quarrying at Greenmoor. The two photographs here were taken at New Biggin Quarry at Well Hill. It is known that stone from Greenmoor was used in the construction of the Wicker Arches and the adjacent Sheffield Victoria Station in 1851. Here, more than fifty workmen pose for the photographer in this 1890s view.

New Biggin Quarry, Greenmoor. A close-up view of the stonemasons at work who are, from left to right: Johnny Wright, George Bramall, J.T. Walton, Percy Illingworth and Harvey G. Thompson.

Farming in the Fox Valley. Prior to the advent of local industry, the area was described as rich meadowland. This location is the field below Stocksbridge Hall (Park Drive) and as such there is a connection with Newtons Farm in Horner House. Harry Newton is holding the horse.

Deepcar allotments. The cultivation of allotments has been a popular pastime for many years. Here we see produce being grown at Mill Lane, Deepcar.

The English Fruit Preserving Company. In 1894, Mr Thomas Oxley obtained the land in that area now occupied by the Swimming Baths and adjacent properties and started a fruit farm to produce raspberries, blackcurrants, gooseberries, plums, damsons, etc. The fruit, when picked, was taken to his factory at Hillsborough. The first of these 1906 views shows a group of willing helpers during a school holiday.

The English Fruit Preserving Company. The collecting tubs on the cart are shown in an upright position and with narrow necks to enable stacking to be done without damaging the fruit.

Underbank Dam. At the end of the nineteenth and the beginning of the twentieth centuries, the growing needs of industry and domestic housing led to the creation of a number of dams. This view from Unsliven Bridge shows Underbank Dam under construction in 1905.

Children of industry. This view has been selected as it shows a group of boys who have evidently just completed a shift in the local pit. It is fitting that we should remember these children of industry whose efforts were so often unfairly demanded of them.

Three

Seats of Learning

Bolsterstone Old School, c.1920. Built in 1686, it was the only school in the area for nearly 200 years. It has also been known as the Free and Endowed School. The teacher in the photograph is Miss Jane Bratt, the children are Jimmy Dyson, Ada Smith and Albert Helliwell. The building is now a private house.

Above: Bolsterstone National School, 1986. Commonly known as Bolsterstone Church School, it was built in 1852. Lessons had to be paid for, so naturally this was not as popular as the Free School. When the two amalgamated in 1886, this building was used for older pupils, the old school for the infants. The fence was erected to protect what remains of the pump which was the public water supply. The school is now a village hall and the schoolhouse is privately owned.

Right: British School, 1922. Extensions to the Ebenezer Chapel were built in 1847 with further extensions added in 1901. It was used until 1929 and headmasters were Henry Jones, Frank Kenworthy, Thomas Vardy. During the 1930s there was an organization called the Young Britons who gave talent shows here.

Below: British School, class 5, of thirty-nine boys, 1925. Back row, left to right: Percy Sellars, Leslie Statham, Alex Pears, Clarence Fletcher, Arthur Eastwood, Arthur White, Herbert Greg, Ernest Withers, Pat O'Hagan. Fourth row: Kenneth Wright, Clarence Webster, Alec Murray, Vernon Morton, Ernest Davies, Bob Shaw, Tommy Milnes, Ernest Rodgers, ? Wright. Third row: Albert Peace, Garfield Hardisty, Hugh Mardlin, Tommy Cox, Bill Whalen, Fred L. Harrison, Jack Staniforth, Ernest Longford, Miss Cree. Second row: Douglas Jones, Tommy Gaines, Eric Eustace, Michael Manion, Charlie Fieldsend, Joe Travis, Jack Brearley. Front row: Joe Woodcock, Donald Evans, Archie Wilson, Leslie Hodgkinkson, Edwin Webster, Albert Kitson.

Opposite below: Bolsterstone National School, c.1924. Cyril Garwood served as headmaster at Bolsterstone before moving to his post at Deepcar. His cricketing pupils are, back row, left to right: Harry Fountain, Leonard Kay, George Thompson, Dan Mate, -?-. Front row: Bob Baker, Herbert Morton, Geoff Hague, George Harry Sampson, Frank Hague, Jack Marsh and Bill Baker

Deepcar School, Carr Road, built in 1856, twenty-two years before St John's Church. An extension was built in 1866 and the infant School in St John's Road in 1896. Headmasters were Mr Cull, Mr Pyrah, Mr Garwood, Mr Jones. When the schools were transferred to the Royd, this site was taken over as an annexe of Stocksbridge College, but has now been converted to private housing. Note the unmade road in this photograph.

Deepcar Junior School, Standard 5, under Mr Harris, 1929. Back row, left to right: Jack Fish, ? Whittaker, Hilda Firth, Ethel Hirst, D. Steward, Mabel Dimmock, -?-. Third row: A. Carter, C. Dickinson, H. Cook, B. Spooner, B. Charlesworth, David ?, R. Jackson, B. Steel, Thora Walton. Second row: B. Dimelow, J. Haller, E. Potts, K. Yeomans, M. Cunningham, E. Kenny, A. Green, P. Wright. First row: L. O'Mahoney, A. Dimelow, M. Askham, A. Gregory, I. Roebuck, K.E. Hanson, R. Shaw, E. Lindley.

The Works School, c. 1910. Built by Samuel Fox in brick in 1867, it was also known as the Red School. In 1910 there were 383 Mixed Juniors and 210 Infants in a building so close to the noise, steam and smoke of the factory and railway that it was hated by all who had to endure it. After 1929 it became part of the Co-op and is remembered as the Tea Rooms.

The Works School, c.1910. It was also known as the Co-op School, and during Mr Bramley's headship, as 'Bramleys'. This may be Mr Bramley in the photograph.

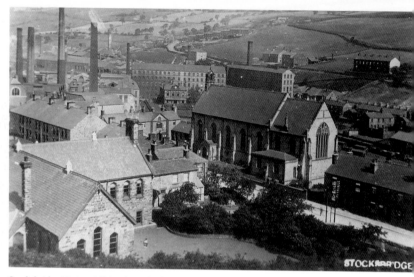

Stocksbridge National School was built in 1868 and used as Day School, Sunday School and Church until St Matthias was built.

Stocksbridge National School, 1894. Mr Swallow was headmaster. Some of the younger ladies would be student teachers. The teacher-pupil ratio seems quite high. By contrast, a 1909 photograph shows one teacher with thirty-three children.

British School, Night School class, 1890s. Back row, left to right: Arthur Dalton, Fred Brown, John Milnes, Sam Andrews, Harry Milnes, Fred Swallow, Arthur Eastwood, Arthur Faulkner, Ernest Marshall. Front: John Howson, Joe Raynor, Albert E. Drabble, Henry Jones.

Ewden Valley School trip. A class of girls believed to be from Deepcar, posing in front of Ewden Village Mission. Pearl Rees is third from the right in the centre row.

Stocksbridge Secondary School, 1929-30. The Barraclough twins, first left on the back row and third left on next row. Leonard was killed in Italy in 1943, serving with the Artillery. Jessie became an S.R.N and nursed in Sheffield Infirmary and in Australia after her husband died.

Stocksbridge Junior School, Cedar Road, 1963-4. The first year after the Junior School's transfer to the purpose-built site off Cedar Road was Mr R. West's last as headmaster. Back row: Barbara Foster, Mrs Pearce, Stuart Hill, Brian Kirbyshaw, Eric Lines, Ruth Hush, Bernadette Green and Alan ?. Front row: Mrs H. Wiseman, Margaret Donkersley, Jean Woodhead, Ron West, Phyllis West, Margaret Dobson and Enid Thompson.

Four

Hassocks and Cassocks

'The Five Worthies'. From left to right: Robert Lievesley, Joseph Hepworth, Reverend Henry Robertshaw, Henry Jones and Mr Moxon. These five men had considerable influence on the lives of people in our valley. All were deacons of the first chapel in Stocksbridge (the Ebenezer), Rev. Robertshaw being the priest there for many years. Mr Jones was the schoolmaster at the British School and all five men played a part in the Stocksbridge Band of Hope Co-operative movement. They encouraged education for both children and adults, and encouraged close connections with industry. The photograph was taken in 1906 on Rev. Robertshaw's eightieth birthday.

Bolsterstone Old Chapel. There has been a chapel or church on this site since 1409, the one in the picture being built in 1791 by the Rev. Thomas Bland. It contained 'spacious galleries, high-backed pews and a three-decker pulpit', quite an achievement for a small rural community.

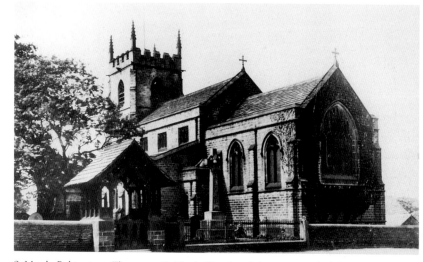

St Mary's, Bolsterstone. The present St Mary's Church at Bolsterstone was built between 1872 and 1879 at a cost of about £7,000. The clock, a gift from the Rimington-Wilson family of Broomhead Hall, and the peal of eight bells, bought by subscription, were dedicated in 1892.

Bolsterstone's peal of eight bells, cast by Taylor and Co. of Loughborough, arrive at Deepcar station prior to their journey up the hill to the church by wagon and horses. The tenor bell alone weighed 12 cwt.

Benjamin Kenworthy is seen here sitting against the 'stone' in Bolsterstone churchyard. Tradition says that this stone is the basis of the place-name 'Bolsterstone' although this is open to question. Note the absence of the lych-gate erected in 1897 to commemorate Queen Victoria's Diamond Jubilee.

The first purpose-built place of worship in Stocksbridge was the Ebenezer Chapel built in 1827. Originally a single-storey building, it had an extra ten feet added to its height in 1847. The main focus of its use gradually changed from worship to education and from 1876 to 1929 it became a day school. After that time it had many functions including those of a meeting house, library and clinic. It was demolished in the early 1960s to make way for shops.

Midhope Chapel of St James the Less was built in the fourteenth century by the Barnbys who were Lords of the Manor. It was restored in 1705. It still retains its box pews and gallery, much of the wood being local oak. The hinges and fastenings were made from local iron ore and the original glass would have been made at the Bolsterstone Glass House.

St John the Evangelist's Church at Deepcar was built in 1878 as a daughter church to St Mary's, Bolsterstone. Prior to it being built, services had been held in Deepcar National School in Carr Road. This building can be seen on the extreme right of the photograph.

St John's Boys Choir, c.1935. Choirs were very popular in the valley, particularly male voice choirs. Back row: Ernest Garner, Brian Ward, Fred Scholey, Eric Firth, Wilson Carter, Harry Ridal, Cyril Robbins, Wilf Staniforth. Third row: Jim Woodcock, Harry Broadbent, Alf Bonner, Jack Newton, Eric Cook, Stanley Ellis, Harold Birks, Arnold Shaw, Jack Shaw. Second row: Alec Herbert, Stan Jackson, organist, Mr Rouse, Rev. Post A.C.L.D., choirmaster, Cyril Garwood, Harry Duffield, Roland Allot. Front row: Alwyn Hill, Brian Booth, Douglas Crossland, Peter Schofield.

The Church of St Matthias, Stocksbridge was opened on 1 November 1890 and cost about £4,200 to build. The foundation stone had been laid by Samuel Fox's son, William Henry, on 8 March 1889 and it was in his father's memory that many of the subscriptions to the cost of building the church were made.

The All Souls Mission, Garden Village, near Oxley Park was originally a fruit store or stable for Oxley's fruit farm. It was acquired by Stocksbridge parish in 1926 to serve a growing population in times of hardship during a National Strike. It was used as a community centre until 1986. Similarly, All Saints Mission, Smithy Moor, was administered by Stocksbridge Parish Church and used continuously until 1989.

The foundation stone to the Wesleyan Chapel, Old Haywoods, was laid in 1867 by the Rev. John Bedford. The builder was Mr J. Brearley of Bradfield and the Chapel opened in 1868. Prior to its building, church services had taken place in a cottage on Bacon Row, Wood Royd.

The Congregational Church, Horner House. The building, now known as the United Reform Church, was built by Mr Ridal and opened in 1864 as the Salem Chapel. This followed a rift between members of the Ebenezer Chapel. The two chapels reunited into this building in 1882. Much of the building was destroyed by fire on 16 November 1921, but was later refurbished.

The 'Whit Monday Sing', c.1906. Whitsuntide was one of the most important periods on the church calendar, culminating in the 'Whit Monday Sing'. All the local churches would march to their respective meeting points, usually with a band or two, and have an interim sing before marching on to join the others. It was also a time for 'new' clothes and an opportunity to meet up with friends as well as a day off work - a rare occurrence for many in our valley.

Whit Monday Whites, c.1906. The Congregational Chapel Sunday School follow their banner through Old Haywoods on their way to the meeting place at Deepcar. It was traditional that the girls wore white and the clothes were always 'new'.

The first 'sing' of the day, c.1906. The Deepcar 'triangle' at the top of Vaughton Hill was usually the meeting place for the first sing of the day.

Following the banner, c.1906. Each church had its own banner and it was customary to rotate the order of churches in the procession each year so that no-one would feel hard done by.

Whit Monday and Peace, 1918. Meanwhile, the Stocksbridge Churches were marching and singing their way along the road towards Deepcar. Here in 1918 they are passing St Matthias Church carrying ensigns as well as the usual banners.

Whitsuntide gathering, c.1906. On meeting, the Stocksbridge, Bolsterstone and Deepcar contingencies all marched to the cricket ground at Bracken Moor, assembled around their respective Sunday School banners (Congregational and Primitive Methodists here) and prepared for a 'reight good sing'. Four of the local dignitaries are seated at the front; the Reverend Henry Robertshaw is second from the left. This photograph shows the gathering at the top of Nanny Hill.

Five

Parades, Carnivals and Gatherings

Peace Day Parade, 1919. During July and August 1919 there were several events in the valley to mark peace after the First World War. This long procession is marching from Deepcar to Stocksbridge, St Matthias Church is just coming into view. The gentleman on the pony is probably Mr Trueman, a local councillor.

Angels of Mons. The following four pictures show a selection of decorated floats which took part in the 'Peace Celebrations' of 1919. Most are of children's groups being pulled by two horses. If the rendezvous was Bracken Moor field (as were many gatherings in the valley) they would need two horses to get them up the steep hills!

This wagon contains Boadicea as well as 'representatives' from the armed services. The horses are being led by members of a Pierrot troupe who were well known in the area.

56

St John's, Deepcar is the name of both the church and the school so it is difficult to know which institution these girls represented. Their well-garlanded wagon must have been a colourful sight.

Peace Day, Deepcar. A report of the events of 19 July 1919 in the Penistone Almanack states, 'Procession on an elaborate scale, free dinner for children, aged people and soldiers, sports, displays by Boy Scouts and Girls' Life Saving Brigade, vocal items by Stocksbridge Junior Choir and Choral Union, and fireworks.' Quite a day!

'Stocksbridge Welcomes Home the Lads.' This concert took place in Fox Glen on 16 August 1919 as part of the Peace Celebrations. Fox Glen is an area of land which was given to the valley by Samuel Fox and Co. in 1911 to commemorate the coronation of King George V and Queen Mary and has been the scene of many concerts and events.

The 'Flat Cap Brigade'. Although we are unable to identify this group of men, nor can we say where exactly the photograph was taken, such a wonderful array of flat caps should not be missed! Many of the men are wearing buttonholes similar to those worn in the peace parades of 1919, hence its inclusion here.

Stocksbridge Carnival, 1926. For many years Stocksbridge had an annual carnival complete with bands, decorated floats and fancy dress parades. Here we see Stocksbridge Old Brass Band about to march from Unsliven Road. Note the 'motor bus' in the background and a crane on the far right.

The Romany wagonette at the third annual carnival. A report in the Penistone Almanack says that the fourth annual carnival had '...many excellent tableaux and fantastic costumes... extending about a mile'. Despite it being 'marred by a heavy thunderstorm' it raised £80, a lot of money in 1928.

A gathering of the Congregational Sisterhood in fields near the Pot House, c.1910. In the middle row, the second from the left is Mrs Jones, and the third from the left is Mrs Hepworth. Mrs Sackett is the fourth from the right on the back row.

The 'worthies' of Stocksbridge and district are gathered together to celebrate the eightieth birthday of Rev. Henry Robertshaw, himself one of the most notable 'worthies' in the valley, in 1906. On the front row from left to right are, fourth, Dr W. Robertshaw, sixth, Joseph Moxon, seventh, Henry Jones, eighth, Rev. H. Robertshaw, tenth, Robert Lievesley, eleventh, Joseph Hepworth.

Six

Local Enterprise

Manchester Road, Stocksbridge.

Stocksbridge Shopping Centre, c.1920. On the south side of Manchester Road are Tommy Farr's outfitters, later Healey's shoe shop, Walker's store with a bakery at the rear, and the Co-op Central stores, grocery and butchery. On the north side are Shentall's grocery, Abson's stationery and hardware, Bramwell's boot and shoe shop, Drabble's Music Shop, Webb's jewelers and the Co-op dry-goods.

Left: Mrs Thickett, c.1910. Minnie and her husband Edwin Thickett both came from Dodworth after their marriage to set up in business in the premises which their granddaughter and her husband still occupy. Edwin was a tailor and she was a dressmaker. She was renowned for her dress sense, especially her large hats. The shop was opened early on Whit Mondays to sell ribbons, gloves and straw bonnets for the Whitsuntide Parade.

Below: Thicketts Shop. The shop opened in 1895 and closed down in its centenary year, when Mr and Mrs McKay retired.

Opposite above: Hunter's Teashop and Friendship Hotel. Hunter's is now Smith Wilkinson's tailors. The new Friendship Hotel was built in 1903 on the site of an earlier one, run by Harriet Battye in 1868-71 and by Elijah Askew in 1881. Tom Battye was the only member of the Local Board not a farmer and the only one to object to the sale of the town's water rights to Sheffield Water Board. He owned the land opposite and had a football team which played there.

Opposite below: T. Farr of Sheffield. This Stocksbridge branch of the Sheffield outfitters was on the south side of the Manchester Road. The manager standing in the doorway is Tom Abson. It was also a pawnshop.

Above: Abson, newsagent. Mr and Mrs Abson sold hardware, sweets and stationery. At Christmas the display windows above the shop were set out with toys and a model railway. The 1905 Trade Directory advertised their 1d Bazaar. Judging by the added name to the shop sign, a new partner had been taken on.

Left: Mr and Mrs Abson. Mrs Abson and her sisters were milliners. After retirement they lived on Linden Crescent, Stocksbridge. Mrs Abson's maiden name was Bella Hepworth.

Opposite below: G.C. Knowles. The Knowles family are one of the very few tradespeople who have maintained a continuous line of business in the area up to the present day. In the early twentieth century it was also profitable to provide transport and cater for weddings and funerals. The horses and wagonettes were stabled in the rear of the premises. The ladies of the family would look after the shop while the men saw to the horses.

Above: G.C. Knowles' first shop on the south side of Manchester Road. They were initially fruiterers and florists, and made wreaths for funerals. Marsden's chemist shop was then east of the Post Office, which was run by Joe Hepworth, printer and newsagent. What is left of this block of buildings is now the Augustus Barnett off-licence.

ARTHUR DRABBLE,
Musical Instrument Dealer,
MOZART HOUSE, STOCKSBRIDGE.

Pianofortes

By Chappell, and other noted makers.

ORGANS by Ferrand, Mason & Hamlin.

Violins, Bows, Melodions, Concertinas, Mandolines, Strings, Music Stands, Cases, Stools, Insulators, and Fittings of all kinds. Repairs of all descriptions done on the Premises. SINGLE TUNINGS or by Yearly Contract. LESSONS given on the Pianoforte and Organ.

PHONOGRAPHS, GRAMOPHONES, FLOWER HORNS, CYLINDER & DISC RECORDS.

NEEDLES AND FITTINGS STOCKED.

LADIES' and GENTS' UMBRELLAS made on the Premises,

Or to order with Fox's Special Tubes   Good Variety of Fit-ups kept.

Re-covering and Repairing done at Reasonable Prices.

VARIED STOCK OF LADIES' AND GENTS' WALKING STICKS.

Arthur Drabble, Mozart House. Originally a dealer in all kinds of musical instruments and fittings, as advertised in the Stocksbridge Almanac of 1910. Arthur Drabble acquired the first motor bike in the district, and we can see by the window display below, extreme left, that the shop began to stock bicycles. His daughter gave piano lessons.

John Webb, Jeweller, 506 Manchester Road, Stocksbridge. J. Webb moved across to the north side of the road, (probably when the new Post Office opened on the corner of Johnson Street), selling watches, clocks and jewellery. The business was later taken over by Woods and more recently by the TSB Bank, which has now closed. T. Bramwell's shoe shop can be seen beyond it, which is now a greeting card shop.

J. Webb, stationer and postmaster. On the south side of Manchester Road was Stocksbridge's first Post Office. That is J. Webb himself at the shop door who sold newspapers, wallpaper and fancy goods. His predecessor as post master was Joseph Hepworth. The poster is proclaiming War News and mentions Mr Chamberlain. The chemist was Marsden's.

Stocksbridge Hawke Green. T.J. Farr, Furniture Dealer, used one of the little wooden shops which always seem to have existed between the stone-built houses, some of which are still occupied, and the more substantial shops to the west. A footpath ran down between the two gable end buildings, as it still does, to Hawke Green Farm opposite the Works gate at the bottom of Smithy Hill.

F. Rickitt, Draper, Manchester Road. F. Rickitt advertised himself as Draper and Milliner - over the shop it also says hosier. These old terms for clothing may soon disappear entirely. These houses were known as Grosvenor Place - two more are at the rear. They were built by Samuel Fox for the people displaced from Hawke Green Farm by the building of the works railway.

Horner House shops. While on the south side of the main road, all the old houses and farm buildings have been replaced by Newton Grange nursing home and the Fire Station. Very little on the north side has changed.

The Beer-Off, Common Piece. This corner-shop served the same area with the same goods for perhaps a century, only closing quite recently. Victoria Road was known as Low Road previously, because funeral processions would go that way to Bolsterstone to avoid the steeper hill. You can see the handrail at the top of Victoria Street where the steps were.

A neighbourhood shop. Smith's' Grocer and Confectioner was on Smith Road, Stocksbridge.

G. Knowles, Wood Willows. Godfrey Knowles, Tailor and Outfitter, occupied the premises which are now solicitors offices on Manchester Road, Deepcar.

The Sportsman's Arms, Haywoods. This public house has been known as Pladdeys after a popular and public spirited couple who were landlords for thirty-eight years. It was a rendezvous for many local organizations. Thomas Pladdey was a renowned angler. His wife ran a soup kitchen during the General Strike. They retired in 1949. The building is now a private house.

The Police Office, Deepcar. The West Riding Constabulary noticeboard bears a recruiting advertisement for footguards. In 1881 there were three policemen living in Stocksbridge between the Coach and Horses and Hawke Green. The station at Deepcar would be the first purpose-built police-house, where the officers could live on the premises. The 1909 Stocksbridge Almanack names a Sgt. Joseph Vardy and five officers.

The Call Office, Deepcar, pre-1907. There were two telephones in the district, one at Samuel Fox and the other for public use in this building next to the Police Station, now the Post Office. By 1908 there were also Call Offices at the Royal Oak, the Coach and Horses and the Friendship Inn.

Deepcar shops, pre-1915. There was a bank just this side of the shops under the awning. The shop at the bottom of Carr Road was at that time J. Robbins, Fancy Goods, Draper and Milliner. In the 1851 Census there were three publicans at Deepcar, all also farmers, but only the Royal Oak was so recorded. There was a blacksmith's in the building on the near right. Horses were still used extensively.

Deepcar Junction, 1860. The earliest known photograph of Deepcar shows the corner shops at the bottom of Carr Road. The Royal Oak Inn had stabling behind - the entry is where we can just see a wagon wheel. The Langsett to Wadsley road had been turnpiked in 1805. People living by a road had to maintain a level, well-drained surface at least twenty feet wide. It was mainly traders who took this responsibility.

The Old Post Office, Deepcar. The building on the left was first used as a Post Office and is now a private house. At the top of Vaughton Hill was a toll-bar, where the public conveniences were until recently. Samuel Fox had to pay 6d for every wagon which passed on its way to Deepcar Station. It was removed in 1872. The shop on the right says G. Hughes, father perhaps of the Tommy Hughes who is still well-remembered.

Travellers' Inn, Vaughton Hill. It was locally known as the Low Drop. The landlord at the time was Arthur J. Reddish, who paid a peppercorn rent to the Lord of the Manor. It was closed in 1920 and is now private property. In 1851 the landlady or publican was called Vaughton.

When "Rag Harry" tak's 'em.!!

Rag Harry. Harry Lockwood was born in 1838 and was hawking needles, thread and matches when only 7 or 8 years old. Abandoned by his father, who went to Australia and made his fortune, Harry was content to travel around the area, collecting rags and jam jars in exchange for salt and produce from Midhope Pottery. The photo was taken on the road to Midhope. He was popular with children whom he would put in the sacks hanging on the cart to give them a ride.

Albert Robinson, the 'Pop' Man. The setting is Hawthorn Brook, outside his business premises on Manchester Road, now demolished. He had been in partnership with Schofield, who later set up on his own in Victoria Street. The label on Robinson's bottles showed a stocks and bridge trademark.

Percy Schofield, fish and poultry dealer. Note the laminated leaf springs under the cart; they were probably made in Fox's Spring Department. It was possibly an ancestor of his, James Schofield, who in the 1881 Census was entered as furnaceman and ginger-beer maker at Hawthorn Brook.

Central Stocksbridge. This photo was taken pre-1910 noting the absence of the Co-op Jubilee building on the right hand (North) side of the main road

Ewden village shop. Built as part of the model village, it served the self-contained community of construction workers and their families.

Ewden village shop interior, stacked from floor to ceiling with basic necessities.

Seven

Wholesale and Divi

The Central Stores in Stocksbridge as it looked when it opened in 1863.

The Friendship Hotel and adjacent property in 1910, the pawnbroker's shop having been the location of the first Co-op shop, which was opened in early 1860.

Another look at Central Stores and adjacent properties. This site is currently occupied by the Sheffield and District Co-operative Society Ltd Grocery Department. The end of Vicoria Street can be seen in the background.

Deepcar Branch (opened in 1893) and adjacent cottage property. The business joining onto the Co-op was a bank.

Old Heywoods Branch, 1910, with the Grocery section and Butchers shop.

Co-op style window dressing showing a good variety of provisions including Pelaw cake flour and Pelaw metal polish.

Langsett Branch opened in 1898 and closed upon completion of the waterworks.

A group of workmen from the Bakery Department which opened in 1889 and by 1910 was producing 1,000 loaves per week.

The Co-op delivery service which appears to be the bread van, judging by the contents.

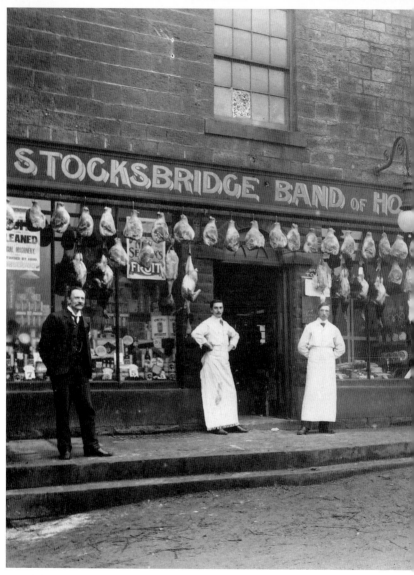

Central Stores, some time after 1906, when Mr D. Massey had been appointed as manager (seen here on the left).

The Manager's House, Victoria Street, Stocksbridge, from a photograph dated to 1910. The site is now occupied by a car park.

A mid-1920s view of central Stocksbridge showing both sections of the Co-op, one on either side of the road. The children will have just come out of the adjacent Works' School.

Preparing for the Co-op procession in 1908. The posters say that in the previous year 38 tons of soap and 13 tons of candles were sold and 504 sheep were killed.

Celebrating fifty years of business at the Jubilee Parade on 2 July 1910, seen here at the bottom of Victoria Street.

Deepcar Branch after the fire which occurred there in the early 1960's.

'Cottage Property and Mineral Water Manufactory at Hawthorn Brook, Near Stocksbridge', as described in Kenworthy's Jubilee History of the Co-op published in 1910. The location is the bottom of Newton Avenue on Manchester Road.

Eight

Fun and Games

Knurr and Spell, Greenmoor. An ancient game which was very popular in the north of England, especially in the West Riding of Yorkshire, in the early twentieth century. Jack Branston's History of Stocksbridge gives a detailed description of it with a photograph very similar to this with all the names. Both show the spade with a name which must have been that of the team sponsor, in this case probably Joel Rusby, landlord of the Rock Inn, Greenmoor. 'Stable' would be the term for a knurr and spell team.

Stocksbridge Church F.C., 1894. The portrait is labelled on the back: Stocksbridge Church Football Club, winners of Sunday School Shield, 1894. It was probably taken in front of the

Old Vicarage on the corner of Haywoods Lane and Bocking Hill, recently demolished. Compare it with the following photograph. Many of the men appear in both.

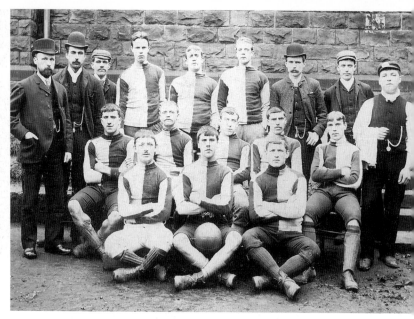

A few of these men have been identified: in the bowler hat on the right, John Sedgwick; the centre player on the back row, Bob Sykes; middle row, first left, a Drabble, second from right, C. Webster; front row, first left, a Dawson; second left, J. Webster.

Opposite below: Stocksbridge Works Victory Club F.C., 1920. The building was erected in 1916 as a Works Canteen. It soon developed into a social club and was named the Victory Club after 1918. Only three of the players have been identified: Vernon Hoyle is second from the left on the back row, Ernest Hance second from the left on the front row and Clarence Lee is the centre forward.

Above: Deepcar United Football Club, c.1910. Third from left in the suit is Ben Walton; first on the right seated is Harry Crossland. Judging by the number of extant team portraits alone, football was the most popular sport. Every pub, club or church had its team.

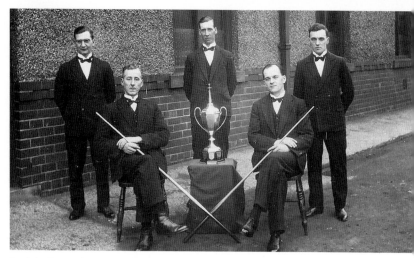

Stocksbridge Works Victory Club. Billiards was more popular then than it is now. This team was Frank Bethel, Frank Whittaker, George Dyson, Walter Sykes and L. Tranter.

Stocksbridge Motorcycle and Light Car Club, 1922. The bow-roofed building was the original 'Peggy Tub' and the bank behind was the site of the War Memorial. The riders were, from left: H. Thompson, E. Hoyland, D. Gregory, W. Hayward, W.H. Clarke, G. Moorhouse, G. Burrows, G. Branston, W. Sutton, T. Fallows, R. Bower and H. Ellison.

Stocksbridge Arundel Club, 1915. This bowling club was started by Dan Emley on Rundle Road, where the children's playground is now. It only lasted a few years and was superseded by that on land between Pot House Lane and Linden Crescent, acquired by Stocksbridge Works Social Services.

Stocksbridge Ladies Bowling Club, 1936. Mrs Annie Emley is second from left on the back row, fourth is Doris Marsh, then Mrs Frances Crossland, and Mrs Moorhouse. Seated are Mrs Adams, captain Mrs Bird and Mrs Elliot. The Bowling Club became part of the Stocksbridge Works Social Services and still thrives.

Stocksbridge Tennis Club, 1920s. It began as a private club, founded by Dr McIntyre, on land adjoining the Bowling Club on Linden Crescent, and was subsequently taken over by Stocksbridge Works Social Services in about 1932. Bob Hance is first left with Dr. McIntyre second left and Tommy Oates far right. The lady on the left is Dorothy (Dolly) Thickett who became Mrs Hance in 1924, and next to her is Bessie Hampshire.

Hockey club, c.1920. Hockey seems to be one of the few games which could be played by a mixed team. There was a club based at Uskers Farm, Deepcar, in 1910, but this photograph is thought to be of a works (S. Fox?) team. Second from right at the back is Fred Aykroyd and first on the right at the front is George Hepworth.

Stocksbridge Evening School Hockey. Shay House Lane School was at the time, and for a long time after, known as the New School. Youngsters who had just left school at 14 had to attend Night School. The teacher is Jack Gwilliam, and next to him Ron Beaumont, Arthur Eastwood, Myra Robinson, Doris Hayward, Oswald Armitage, Arnold Eastwood and Clifford Batty. At the front a girl called Hill, Rene Sackett, Fred Aykroyd (coach), Ethel Copley and Jessie Eastwood.

Stocksbridge Works hockey, c.1932. The ground is probably Bracken Moor. The first player on the back row is Colin Castledine.

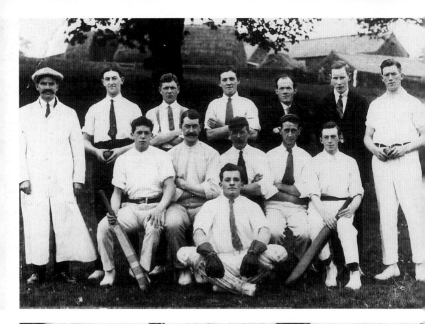

H.Whittaker
Photo-Lithographer

Langsett United F.C. 1923-1924.

Bolsterstone Athletic F.C., 1936-7. Back row, left to right, are Len Creswick, Capt. Wilson, Oswald Dyson, Bill Dawson, Geoff Hague, Jack Marsh, George Harry Sampson, Roland Shaw, and Rev. Holt. Front: Bill Dimelow, Jim Shaw, Colin Jackson, Joe Haley, Harry Hague and Thomas C. Hinde.

Opposite above: Midhope Cricket Club, 1921. The umpire is David Bramall. Third from the left, standing is Percy Hirst. Seated are Harold Roberts, John Mate, Mr Roberts, Jarvis Thickett. Centre front is Clarence Cherry, and standing with the ball, Bill Grayson.

Opposite below: Langsett United Football Club, 1923-4. Billy Green, landlord of the Wagon and Horses, or Langsett Inn, used to pay men from outside the village to play, and of course, entertained them all to a good meal after the game. Clarence Cherry is second from left at the back, 'Nigger' Whittaker on the extreme right. Seated first left is Joe Mills, and on the extreme right Harold and Percy Roberts.

Stocksbridge Old Cricket Club, founded 1862. Taken in 1950 on the occasion of the Vice-Presidents' Day, showing many veteran players with Oliver Inman, chief engineer at S. Fox, benefactor and supporter of many sports in this valley. Back row, left to right: Herbert Marsden, John Spooner, Reg Jagger, Herbert Hance, Ron Corbet. Third row: Charlie Gaskell, Arnold Hitchen, Jack Booth, Henry Woodhead, Joe Eastwood, Norman Fawcett, Harry Puttigill, Jack Walton. Second row: Eric Heath, Jack Hanwell, Freddie (Bob) Taylor, 'Walshie' Gill, Bill Price, Harry Parkin, Dick Day, Harry Eastwood, Fred Woodcock, Harry Walton sen., Johnny Booth. Front row: Harold Wright, Arthur Eastwood, Ernest Ashton, Horace Bradbury, Oliver Inman, Jack Eastwood, Robert Copley, Bob Copley. Jack Hanwell provided meat and potato pies.

Stocksbridge Golf Club, 1929-30. Another private club, founded in 1924 by Jack Kilbride and others at Townend, Deepcar, it has remained so. The original clubhouse was a small wooden hut, replaced by this brick and pebble-dash building in 1929. Among this group relaxing outside the new clubhouse are Douglas and Edna Heath, both second from left. Mrs Heath, now 92, is a life member and still very interested in golf. Centre back is Mr Eastwood and far right is Billy Hanwell.

Stocksbridge Golf Club, 1966. The occasion was Lady Captain's Day. Back row, left to right: Connie Woodhead, Norah Barlow, Joyce Whalen, Mary Langley, Doris Elliot, Barbara Skinner, Sylvia Wright and Mary Corbridge. Middle row: Jenny Drabble, Annie Robinson, Jean Senior and Mrs D. Skinner. Front row: Mary Fish, Kath Hingley, Doreen Wormleighton, Muriel Senior, Rosie Knowles (Capt.), Doris Hough, Margery Hamon, Betty Oxspring and Doris Barlow.

Nine

Leisure and Pleasure

Merrie England. Fred Swallow was a leading player in the production of *Merrie England* by St Matthias Operatic Society in 1928.

Above: St Matthias Operatic Society, c.1928. Rehearsals were held in the Church School. The conductor was Clarence Elliot. Jim Addy, headmaster, was director and scene-painter. Mrs Mary Whittaker was secretary and, on this occasion, stand-in actress. Back row: A.F.C. Foster, Mary Whittaker, Elsie Pickering, Annie Swallow, (Mary's sister) and Alice Drabble (Mrs S. Henderson). Middle row: Gladys Gill, Maude Rolfe and Ilene Rees (Mrs A. Whitworth). Front: Rupert Haigh.

Below: Follies Troupe, c.1920. The setting of this portrait is of equal interest. The building on Edward Street, Stocksbridge, was originally owned by Schofields and was used for the Electric Cinema, the first Salvation Army meetings, Tiny Eastwood's dancing classes and furniture exhibitions. It is now the British Legion club. The troupe was a charitable organisation.

Stocksbridge Ladies Jazz Band, c.1933. This band included Deepcar youngsters, some of them boys. They rehearsed and held concerts in the Miners' Welfare Hall. This group included Joan Mills, Melba Sutton, Evelyn Pearson, Gertie Brookes, Zilla Jubb, Olive Wragg and "Taffy" Jenkins.

Deepcar Follies, c.1935. This was a concert group organised by a few Deepcar parents. Proceeds were given to church and school funds in rotation. Back row: Gordon Stainrod, Eric Cook, Stanley Jackson and Harry Duffield. Third row: Jack Newton, Bessie Woodcock, Joyce Fieldsend, Joyce Jackson, Margaret Armitage, Joyce Hanwell and Jim Woodcock. Second row: Elsie Cook, Jean Goodison, Joyce Barraclough, Hilda Duffield, Elsie Revill, Joan Stafford and Peggy Cheetham. Front row: Ken Gregory, Enid Haigh, Cynthia Bull and Jack Butcher.

Stocksbridge Brass Band, 1896. The Old Brass Band is one of the earliest institutions in the district, having been founded in 1851. Samuel Fox took an interest and provided a set of top-class instruments. When these needed replacing local fund-raising allowed purchase of three sets

at a cost of £1,000. The Umbrella Workshop at S. Fox Ltd was used for practice and later, the Rod Mill. A professional tutor visited and would stay overnight; members were keen enough to meet in the Hive Yard at 7 a.m. on the Sunday morning before he left.

STOCKSBRIDGE OLD BRASS BAND 1934

Stocksbridge Brass Band, 1934. Names associated with the band's earliest days are John Jeffrey, John Simpson, J. & A. Micklethwaite, Charles Thickett, James Charlesworth, George Marsden and Robert Dawson. The 1934 Band: back row, left to right: F. Bacon, N. Emmerson, J. Firth, A.Ross, T. Collier, G. Travis, W. Willows. Second row: J. Kaye. H. Dyson, J. Horton, L. Milnes, D. Poyser, H. Marsh, W. Hodgkinson, E. Marshall and F. Smith. Front: W. Midgley, O. Travis, J. Slater, J. Bacon, C. Fish, H. Taylor, W. Faulkner, J. Sach and J. Midgley.

Opposite below: Les Buxton's Band, 1938. This popular dance band played throughout the war years and afterwards at the Victory Club Saturday night dances, the annual Police Ball, Tradesmen's Ball, etc. Pictured are A. Hayward, P. Milnes, L. Sheldon, J. Marsh, E. Webster, L. Buxton, L. Milnes and G. Bowden.

Above: Stocksbridge's Popular Dance Band. Alan Ross played trumpet, Herman Gill was drummer, Harry Hance was the pianist, Fred Laycock played the violin, and Arthur Barden performed on the banjo.

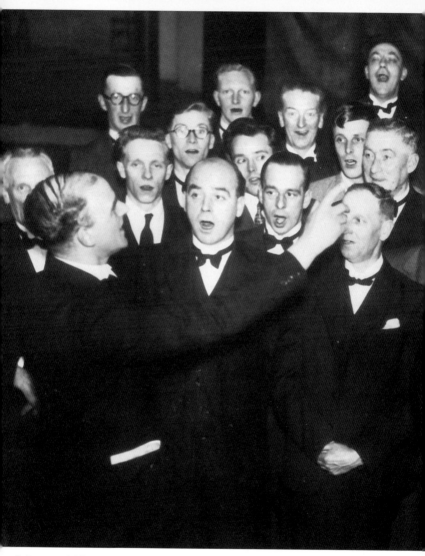

Bolsterstone Male Voice Choir, 1948. The remaining members of the Bolsterstone Male
Voice Choir practised with their conductor William Evans shortly after the tragic accident at
Holmfirth which cost the lives of six of their members, two of their wives and the coach driver.
Several were injured. Back row: Willis Hague, F. Copley, H. Marsden, K. Hodgkinson, H.

Haigh, V. Firth, A. Firth, A. Halliwell. Middle row: R. Davis, R. Elliot, D. Dyson, J. Gillot, D. Cherry, B. Hodgkinson, E. Cooke, J. Ellison, A. Sampson, L. Creswick. Front row: C. Saunders, E. Firth, V. Hardisty, T. Cooke, T. Wainwright, B. Dobson, R. Sanderson, E. Staniforth, H. Lowe.

Stocksbridge Senior School Choir. On 6 May 1938 these children participated in a Music Festival at the Royal Albert Hall, London. Back: Eric Firth, William Haigh, William Pollard, Alec Herbert, Ruby Wood. Third row: Doreen Dyson, Joan Stafford, Betty Jennings, Elaine Matthews, Joyce Booth. Second row: Margaret Faulkner, Joan Robinson, Dulcie Bancroft, Jean Ridal, Christine Marsh. Front: Brian Trickett, Brian Rogers, Robert Levitt, the last boy has not been identified.

Opposite below: Stocksbridge First Scouts. Lord Somers, accompanied by Capt. Harold West, inspecting a parade of Stocksbridge First Scout Group on the occasion of the opening of a new Scout Hut in Hole House Lane on 12 July 1941. The hut was demolished a few years ago.

Above: Deepcar St John's Church Guides. Back row: Margaret Broomhead, Peggy Cheetham, Dorothy Turner, Sarah Nielson, Diana Willey and Edith Hudson. Middle row: Dora Slater, Doreen Hall, Vera Beever, Annie Ridal, Joy Barraclough, Jean Garwood, Hilda Duffield and Elsie Cook. Front row: Hilda Lawton, Joan Robinson, Margaret Dimmock, Peggy Trueman, Rev. S.R. Post, Peggy Robinson, Joan Stafford and Bessie Woodcock.

Left: Stocksbridge Cycling Club, 1940s. Reg Clark, Neil Lindley, Eric Rutledge.

Below: W.E.A. Ramblers. Celia Hepworth and Enid Atkinson are Stocksbridge girls amongst this group of ramblers, which includes members from the Barnsley area. Cyclists and walkers thought nothing of travelling to join up with others to set off into the countryside.

Ten

On the Move

Deepcar Station. The station was originally opened in 1845 but was subsequently rebuilt as shown in this and following photographs in 1865. This view is dated 1910. When first opened, the station was part of the Manchester, Sheffield and Lincolnshire railway which was renamed the Great Central Railway after the London extension to Marylebone was completed in 1899. The bay platform was the terminus for the Stocksbridge Railway Co. passenger service.

A rare external view of the station buildings showing the tranquility of the end of the nineteenth and the beginning of the twentieth centuries. The presence of the transport suggests that a train is due to arrive.

Deepcar Station looking towards Wortley, c.1910. The connection with the Stocksbridge Railway Co. is through the cutting to the left of the distant signal. The place-name signs read 'Deepcar for Stocksbridge'.

In 1877, the Stocksbridge Railway Co. Ltd was opened to give a connection with the local steelworks and the Manchester, Sheffield and Lincolnshire Railway at Deepcar. This locomotive was built by Hudswell Clarke in 1910.

S. Fox and Co. Ltd locomotive no. 4, built in 1907 and looking new here after being supplied in May at a cost of £1504.

Another Fox loco of approximately 1910 vintage.

Another view of loco no. 4 taken at the works some years later. This locomotive was built by Hudswell Clarke (Number 808) with outside cylinders of 15-inch diameter and 22-inch stroke, boiler pressure 160 p.s.i. and a 6-feet wheel base. It was eventually scrapped in 1950.

Opposite below: During 1913-14 a railway was built in Ewden Valley to assist with the construction of the dams. The line crossed the Sheffield-Manchester road at More Hall and connected with the Great Central Railway near to Wharncliffe Wood signal box. The saloon coach is believed to be ex-Lancashire and Yorkshire Railway, 1870, and was used for the passenger service in the valley.

Above: A busy scene at the sidings within Fox's Works. The carriage is of interest, as this would have been used to carry passengers on the Stocksbridge Railway to Deepcar.

Horse-drawn fire engine on display at a local show, c. 1920. The vehicle is marked 'Urban District Council'.

A later model, probably 1930s vintage. The original fire-station was behind the Town Hall. Later it was transferred to the building behind the cinema, before its relocation to the present site at Horner House.

Opposite above: Motorised wheel chair for Mr Clarke of Scotch Row who was severely disabled as a result of an accident in the steelworks.

Opposite below: A vintage Rudge motor bike of unknown date. The two gentlemen are Eli Shaw, on the bike, and his passenger, Chell Whittaker.

Revill, Sons and Broadbent, 1924-30. John William Revill began as a small-holder and carter, distributing his own produce but also working on Underbank Reservoir and for Samuel Fox & Co. He would transport a load of steel bars to Birmingham, a twenty-four hour journey. In 1901 he was a greengrocer; he would take his cart to Glen Howe, Wharcliffe Side, selling ice-cream. This photograph would have been taken between 1924-1930. At weekends and holidays, the

flat-bed was converted to this charabanc with removable side-panels. There was also a waterproof hood, tailored by William Machon. The vehicle was garaged up Ash Lane, while the firms office was situated on Manchester Road, Old Haywoods. The business transferred later to the Ive Yard, Deepcar, where he had lived as a boy.

Percy Schofield's first coach. This view was taken at the top of Smithy Hill in the early twenties. The Town Hall caretaker, Fred Newton, who lived in the house in the background, kept a lovely rose garden behind the Town Hall.

Opposite below: A landau and pair belonging to the Knowles business.